WHAT BEND? I CAN'T EVEN SEE THE ROAD!

James Tanis

James Tanis
Isaiah 42:3

An Eight Week Bible Study for Small Groups or Individuals

DEDICATION

To my amazing wife, Kimberly, my rock,

and to my boys, Zechariah and Jacob,

who continue to delight and amaze me with their God-given talents.

My Life Verse:
"A bruised reed he will not break, and a smoldering candle he will not
snuff out."
--Isaiah 42:3

INTRODUCTION

You are holding a book about hope. Not wishy-washy hope: "I hope things work out for you," or, "I hope I get this right." That is just wishing that everything will be o.k., but you can not really be sure.

The hope of which I speak refers to eternal hope that is only found in God through our Lord, Jesus Christ. As Romans 15:13 says, *"May the God of hope fill you with all joy and peace as you trust in him, so that you may overflow with hope by the power of the Holy Spirit."* Regardless of circumstances, which can strip us of earthly securities, whether health, prosperity, emotional, and other comforts, what cannot be taken from us? Our hope, which is in salvation through Christ.

If you are on this earth, you are going to experience suffering in one degree or another. It is my experience that my perspective toward my suffering makes all the difference. Sometimes I do not feel like responding triumphantly, but it is not about feeling. It is about choice. According to Romans 5:2-5, notice what occurs <u>before</u> hope: *"...And we rejoice in the hope of the glory of God. Not only so, but we also rejoice in our sufferings, because we know that suffering produces perseverance; perseverance, character; and character hope. And hope does not disappoint us, because God has poured out his love into our hearts by the Holy Spirit, whom he has given us."* Hope is the last listed! Who doesn't want a good dose of perseverance and character along the way?

Jeremiah 29:11 says, *"'I know the plans I have for you,' declares the Lord, 'Plans to prosper you and not to harm you, plans to give you hope and a future.'"* Although God was speaking to Israel, who would remain in captivity another seventy years, God is also speaking to all of us. God knows the details of his plans but we do not. However, we are assured that we may trust God's will because his thoughts are for our good, not evil. When we suffer, we have hope because Jeremiah's words reassure us that we have a future because his plans for us are peace, shalom, not harmful things. Don't believe me? Ask Job, who <u>never</u> found out that the suffering he endured was used for the Lord's glory!

Through my journey from perfect health, to near death, and slowly working my way toward health again, I cannot imagine what it would be like to not have the Lord. I heard so many scared, hopeless patients crying out during my several hospital stays. I just prayed for their comfort and thanked God that he knew me and I was learning to know him.

I continually refer to what I call my "life verse" because I can identify with it and it gives me so much hope. My life verse, which is on the dedication page also, is Isaiah 42:3:
"A bruised reed he will not break, and a smoldering candle he will not snuff out." Be blessed with this verse and the following as you prepare to join me on my "life drive:" *"...we who have fled to take hold of the hope offered to us may be greatly encouraged. We have this hope as an anchor for the soul, firm and secure." Hebrews 6:18-19*

TABLE OF CONTENTS

THE SMOOTH, STRAIGHT ROAD

I knew I wanted to be a teacher. I loved kids. I loved my teaching courses at Central Michigan University. I was an ESL (English as a Second Language) teacher in Nanchang, China as well as an underground missionary for the 1990-1991 school year. Yes! This was my passion, my calling! My God-given gift! I was going to teach for at least 30 years, probably more. My wife and I left the relative safety of our native Michigan for our first teaching assignment in the states in Yuma, Arizona. My career and life was seen as far as the long, straight desert highway. If I only knew 20 years later, I would lose my career, and almost my life.

"I can do this," I thought. I had been sitting on the hospital bed for fifteen minutes, convincing my wife, Kim, that I was going for my first walk in over two very long weeks. With her help, I am standing, Kim on my left and the IV stand on my right. Out to the door. Shuffle, shuffle. Turn right. Now walk the longest hospital block in the world. Shuffle, shuffle, stop. Stand. Shuffle, shuffle. Nurses everywhere smiled.

"Mr. Tanis! Oh, Mr. Tanis! You're walking!" I tried to smile, but I could only glance toward the nurses' voices with my blurred vision. I used all my concentration to move my cement legs. Nurses' station, turn left.

"You're doing great, hon," Kim encouraged. "Shouldn't you sit down now?" I mumbled and willed my wooden feet to shuffle onward. It was considerable time inching to that last corner that would take me back to my room.

Creak, phhhh. Creak, phhhh. The sound increased.

"What is that sound?" I asked Kim.

"It's an old man who looks to be in his 90s pushing a walker."

"I an **not** letting that old geezer pass me!" I hissed and forced my left foot up. Clunk. Drag right foot. Clunk. Drag. Chunk. Drag. Chunk. I went through the door of my room, turned, squinted, and smiled at "walker-man." He didn't turn to look at me; he was staring straight ahead, concentrating as I had. After he eventually passed, I asked Kim,

"Wow. He looked bad. I don't look like that, do I?"

"No, you don't," my wife lied, wanting to say that I actually looked worse. I eased my exhausted body back into my hospital bed as Kim lifted my dead legs. The safety of the dark hospital room was comforting. Kim kissed my forehead, and I immediately fell into a hard sleep.

A SOUTHWESTERN DETOUR

It was the summer of 1991 and I had just returned from a year long missionary stint in China. I took myself and my shiny new English teaching degree to Nanchang, China to teach English at a traditional Chinese medical school, where I also lived. Nanchang is the home of Chairman Mao and was the beginning of the Communist uprising. I was part of a small group of Americans were the first to be allowed to teach in this relatively small Chinese city of 2.5 million people. This was also a couple of months after the Communist crackdown in Beijing where over a million pro-Democracy demonstrators were murdered. I have great timing like that. But that is another adventurous story.

A friend from Central Michigan University gave me a tip about a middle school music teacher that was needed in Yuma, Arizona. Since Kim and I could not get jobs on the same side of the state and we were getting married in October, I called the middle school. After a short interview with the principal who enthusiastically gave me the job over the phone, I bravely asked if there were any opening for my fiancée. Before we knew it, we packed our few belongings that only filled half of the smallest U-Haul and drove across the country to new jobs, new lives, and new careers: Kim as a fifth grade teacher and me as a middle school choir director.

Although we now lived on the border of Mexico, we had planned our wedding in Michigan through old-fashioned letter writing while I lived in China. Yes, the internet hadn't really caught on yet. After school on Friday, we flew back to Michigan on the 25th of October, had the rehearsal dinner on the 26th, were married on Sunday the 27th of October, spent one night at the Amway Grand Hotel, flew all night on the 28th and taught that Monday, the 29th.

The things you can accomplish when you're young, energetic, and in L-O-V-E!

LUCK O' THE DUTCH

After six years of teaching in Yuma, and stumbling our way through parenthood with our first born, red headed son, Zechariah, we decided to see if we could get jobs back in Michigan. After dozens and dozens of resumes were sent, we were offered teaching jobs in the rural village of Lakeview, Michigan. We settled in, laid down roots, joined a Free Methodist church, and welcomed Jacob, boy number two.

I continued loving my job and every new group of fourth graders was my best class ever. In late fall of 2007, my legs began to ache deep in my bones. By Christmas, it was more prevalent. In the early spring, my legs and back were affected. I took a hot bath every night to help relax the muscles so I could sleep. By March, I was in constant pain and had been taking three ibuprofen every four hours, night and day for months. I had a fabulous student teacher in the fall of 07, but I was still really struggling to keep up physically with my job.

March 17th, St. Patrick's Day, I realized that I couldn't get up from my desk after school. My wife taught across the hall, so I called her on the phone and she came to help me stand.

"You're going to E.R. right now!"

"No I'm not!"

"Yes, you are, so zip it!"

So, with much effort, we went to the local hospital were I was quickly admitted. My sedimentation rate was 364, the highest ever seen there or any other hospital in the area. A sedimentation rate is a general marker for systemic inflammation. Average folks' rate is around 14. I was asked to lie on my side in fetal position while the doctor performed a lumbar puncture, or spinal tap. I swear that needle was so long that she had to stand in the next room to begin the injection! This ER visit prompted various blood work for viral and bacterial infections, an alphabet soup of acronyms—EKG, EEG, MRI, CAT scan, and more. Mystery of mysteries, they could not know what to do with me, so they sent me home—where my spinal tap leaked, causing even more excruciating pain.

I continued to deteriorate and pass out with pain and be in such misery that two days later I had to be carried to the car, back to ER. The local hospital put me right on an ambulance and transferred me to a larger hospital in Grand Rapids. That ambulance ride was no more comfortable than riding in the back of a pickup truck! I was shocked at how rough it was!

Now that I was admitted to a huge hospital with a lot of doctors and a lot of answers, right?

Not so much.

TAKING PUZZLES OUT OF THE BOX

Elevated levels of troponen indicate a heart attack, so doctors suspect endocarditis, which is inflammation of the heart. I was also anemic, which indicates a chronic disease. Some doctors think it may be a connective tissue disease. Several doctors commented, "This is a real puzzle."

My fever remained very high, as did the joint and muscle pain. Kim came and lightly put her hand on my chest. I rasped, "Don't. I can't breathe." She called the nurse and I went from zero oxygen to the maximum level of six liters. As doctors paraded in and out while I was getting worse, I thought for the very first time, "They don't know what to do. I'm dying. I'm only 40, and I'm actually dying."

To add to my list, I now had pneumonia. I had such a chest heaviness and shortness of breath. Doctors said that this pneumonia was not typical and they had to think outside the box. Doctors even looked for weird fungi from Arizona and China. Another MRI was looking at inflammation of the brain and lymphoma. Cancer along with bone marrow and lung biopsies were discussed with Kim, as well as heavy metal poisoning. Some doctors thought it was adult onset Still's disease, but others disagreed. If they treated me incorrectly, it would kill me. However, doing nothing was also killing me. I was literally racked with pain from head to toe, chock-full of inflammation, with stunning headaches. For untold hours, Kim put cold cloths on my feet and legs. My toes were swollen sausages. The shades were pulled shut and the room was made as dark as possible. Movement around me made me nauseated. I couldn't even have balloons that were sent to me stay in the room.

I would want to see my boys so badly, who were 13 and 10 at the time. My parents would drive them the hour to the hospital, but I would be too sick to even see them.

Tears rolled down my cheeks as I silently cried. Sobbing hurt too much.

When I thought I could take no more, I had a spiritual battle that was as tangible as the book you are holding.

FAITH STOP 1

1.   Have you ever envisioned how your life would be? Has it turned out how your mind's eye saw it, or have things gone differently than planned? Are things better, worse, or just right?

2.   Where did God fit in your life's planning? How long have you been saved? As you reflect, have you relied on God for direction and guidance, or have you planned and, because it's generally good stuff, you can fit God into the plans you already made?

3.   Have you ever had a crisis, whether it was physical like James', emotional, spiritual, or situational, such as loss of job? How did you react to it? Where was God in the crisis?

4.   Ponder the following statement: "When God is all you have, then God is more than enough."

5.   Do you know someone who has held their faith high as they have endured trials? What did they do that showed others that their faith conquered their circumstances?

ROAD TO HELL AND BACK

It began around midnight. My pain level remained very high, but I finally began to doze off while Kim slept in the chair. Suddenly, there was a creature there, flying toward my face. No hair, bat-like wings, large, evil eyes, sharp craggy teeth filled its oversized mouth. Its skinny gray arms reached toward me with sharp pointed fingers. It pulled up right before it would have made contact with my head.

There was another one behind it. And another. And another. All were lunging toward my bed, wide dark mouth open, showing broken sharp teeth. Each one looking as if to devour me head first, but then swooping above my head.

My eyes popped open, but, to my incredulous dismay, the creatures were still there, reaching, swooping up toward my face. Some of these beasts looked male, some female, and most disturbing were the ones that resembled demented children. All were reaching their sharp claw-like fingers, mouths gaping open. I was literally being scared to death.

I wanted to swat at them, but I was too weak to raise my arms. Their swooping was taking my breath away. I barely whispered, "Kim." Again and again I called her name the best I could muster, and she finally roused.

"Help me. Demons. Everywhere. Flying at my face." She ran to my side and asked, "Where?"

She couldn't see this attack? How could she not see them? Kim climbed into bed with me and held my drenched body tightly.

"Help me know what is real. Help me know what is real," I whimpered. The attacks continued for five hours. Kim's prayers stopped the attacks eventually. She held me tightly as if to keep me from being carried away by these demons.

I thought daylight would never come. Although the light hurt my eyes terribly, I was so grateful for it. Kim and a nurse carried my and my IV to the shower where I felt the warm water washing away the dark clingings of an incredibly awful night.

I know this sounds like just a dream or something from a movie. The fact that I was awake and these horrid terrifying demons continued their attacks for hours, I knew this was a real, tangible spiritual attack. I have never seen these demons since that time, and I pray the Lord's protection forever from ever experiencing this again.

FAITHSTOP 2

1. Spiritual attacks are not necessarily as physically seen as James' experience. How do you define a spiritual attack?

2. Read the following verses and comment:

"For we do not wrestle against flesh and blood, but against the rulers, against the authorities, against the cosmic powers over this present darkness, against the spiritual forces of evil in the heavenly places. –Ephesians 6:12

"For though we walk in the flesh, we are not waging war according to the flesh. For the weapons of our warfare are not of the flesh, but have divine power to destroy strongholds. We destroy arguments and every lofty opinion raised against the knowledge of God, and take every thought captive to obey Christ." --2 Corinthians 10:3-5

"Be sober-minded; be watchful. Your adversary the devil prowls around like a roaring lion, seeking someone to devour." --1 Peter 5:8

3. What images do these verses conger up in your mind? Should we interpret these verses literally? Are they exaggerated hyperbole?

4. What are common spiritual battles and temptations everyone faces? What spiritual battles do you face?

"THE MYSTERY MAN" FAILS THE TESTS

My voice, barely audible, asked Kim, "Help me. Why can't I have medicine for this pain?" As more tears fell, she said that I was on morphine, and not a small dose. Extreme, never ending nerve pain changed my perspective. I loved my family. I wanted to grow old with my soul mate, but I desperately wanted this throbbing head to toe pain to stop, even if it meant dying. I was ready to be with the Lord and worship Him in glory. I really was.

I was in and out of consciousness for the next several days, not sure what side of the Jordan on which I would awake. I always woke to astonishing pain and my Kim by my side, cooling my legs with wet towels and tubs of ice water. My IV was removed, causing another terrible night without pain medicine. The IV was reinserted, but because I was dying, my veins were collapsing, taking three nurses and several tries to reinsert the IV needle.

Doctors just called me "The Mystery Man." Viral meningitis or aseptic meningitis was the guess of a few doctors. Some doctors suspected temporal arteritis. The only way to test is for this is to cut out sections of arteries next to each ear. If it tests positive, it is 100% accurate. If it tests negative, well, I could still have it and it was missed. A young doctor was excited at the possibility of this being the diagnosis because I would have been the youngest person ever to be diagnosed with temporal arteritis. He was chomping at the bit to start writing a medical paper starring little ole me. It was a painful procedure and I had to be awake, listening to the scraping, knowing that he was digging into the sides of my head. Much to the young doctor's dismay, the test returned negative. I still have two souvenir scars next to my ears to remind me of that dreadful procedure.

Some doctors wanted to rule out infection of the tricuspid heart valve and endocarditis, so a transesophagal echocardiogram was ordered. You notice the word esophagus in that word? This little treatment meant that I had to swallow what looked like a garden hose with a little camera attached at the end. I was told that they would give me amnesia medicine so I wouldn't remember the procedure. I actually do remember having that hose shoved down my throat and gagging over and over. Good times. That lovely procedure came back fine, so the mystery continued.

The doctors finally knew they had to do something. They agreed to inject high doses of steroids, knowing that if they were wrong, it would kill me, but I was dying in that hospital bed while no treatments were administered.

EASTER MORNING MIRACLE

Praise the Lord, the doctors were right! My sausage toes and red swollen legs began to pulse less. I became more and more conscious and could whisper sentences. I could whisper aloud my thankfulness through The Lord's Prayer, MY Lord's Prayer.

As the high doses of steroids continued to course through my veins, my return to this world seemed miraculous. The constant, vast pulsing throughout my body had lessened, thankfully. A beautiful African-American nurse came in singing a hymn. I thanked her for working on Easter Sunday. She said, "Oh honey, I've been to church already. If Jesus could rise from the dead, the least I can do is get to Sunrise Service before work!" She helped me sit up and dialed the telephone for me.

"Hello, mama."

"I can't believe you're calling!"

"I'm sitting up and feeling o.k."

"This is an Easter miracle!" she sobbed.

My doctor, Dr. Martin, came to see me after his church service. He was a believer, but I still started preaching to him anyway and thanking him and Jesus for saving my life. He shook my hand and laughed, "It is so great to see you smiling and talking, James. I though we were going to lose you."

"Apparently, I've got more work to do here, even though my heart and head were ready to go to Glory."

I read Jeremiah 17:14 and Jeremiah 30: 17 over and over while praising the Lord. Even though I had no appetite and every thing tasted like sand, I choked down some Jell-o and was forced to drink Ensure. Blech. Liquid sand. What a wonderful, wonderful Easter that was!

FAITHSTOP 3

1. The doctors took their best guess in bringing James back from the brink of death. On a less dramatic note, what decisions have you made based on your "best guess" with the information you had?

2. Consider Proverbs 3:5-6 *"Trust in the Lord with all your heart, and do not lean on your own understanding. In all your ways acknowledge him, and he will make straight your paths."* Do you ask God for guidance with your big decisions? What about smaller ones?

3. How can you apply this verse to your life? *"So, whether you eat or drink, or whatever you do, do all to the glory of God."* *1 Corinthians 10:31*

4. Look up Jeremiah 17:14 and Jeremiah 30: 17 and read the words aloud. How are these hopeful verses for a believer?

DRIVING HOME

Ouch! What hurt more than taking out that thick IV needle? Ripping off the tape! I'm a hairy guy and that super sticky tape left a bald red spot on my arm! I quickly got over it when I realized that I wasn't attached to that beep, beep, beeping IV machine. Wahoo! Now I could walk around freely! Oh yeah, I couldn't really walk, but I had a shiny new hundred dollar walker on which to learn.

The smell of food was absolutely nauseating. The cafeteria kept delivering plates of food, but I would beg Kim or my parents to take it out in the hallway so my stomach would stop rolling. I was still semi-agreeing to suck down chocolate-sandy Ensure. Even so, I entered the hospital at 165 pounds and was now leaving less than 130 pounds. My muscle tone just melted away. What a difference two weeks can make.

A nurse and Kim helped my emaciated body into a wheelchair. Finally, I was being discharged! Down the elevator, out the door, and into the car. It felt so good to see that hospital disappear in the background.

After an hour, we turned on our dirt road and Kim started sobbing. I looked at her quizzically. She said, "I honestly did not think I would ever be bringing you home. Thank God for this day."

Driving down the driveway was a breath of fresh air. Home. Safety. I thought, "I'm going to be all right." I smiled, or at least I tried. I was so exhausted that I had to consciously think to keep my head up.

This was also the day that was scheduled for my two male alpacas to be delivered. Having alpacas had been a dream of mine for several years. I had researched them and visited several farms, and had a couple of Amish buddies build a small barn and fence in an acre to house them. Kim had told me in the hospital two days before that she was canceling the delivery, but I begged her, "Please don't take this away from me. I've lost so much. I need them." Even though I couldn't take care of them, she answered, "Of course."

The alpacas were delivered that afternoon. Hank and Little John were secured in their field and things were going to be o.k. Thank you, God, for letting me see this day!

FAITH STOP 4

1. Have you ever had a close call, like slippery driving in the winter? Or an accident where everyone was o.k.? How did you feel after you knew everything was all right? Do you remember any physical reactions? Heart palpitations? Sweating? Crying? Did you call out to God? Thank Him afterward? Discuss.

2. What was Kim's reaction when James was brought home? What do you think your reaction would have been?

3. What words or pictures are invoked when you hear the word "safety?" Why did James choose that word in the fifth paragraph? Why did he make it a sentence unto itself?

4. Do you think verses like this help one's faith in crisis, or make one "bristle" upon hearing these words? *"Consider it pure joy, my brothers, whenever you face trails of many kinds, because you know that the testing of your faith develops perseverance. Perseverance must finish its work so that you may be mature and complete, mot lacking anything." James 1:2-4.*

5. Review and discuss these verses as they apply to the believer's life: Ephesians 1:17, 19, Ephesians 3:16, and Psalm 91:1-2.

HANK AND LITTLE JOHN

The alpaca ranch owners came late the afternoon of my homecoming with my special delivery. I couldn't walk to the alpaca corral even though one of the gates was only a couple hundred feet down the driveway. My family walked me/carried me to the car and we drove down the driveway to talk to the husband and wife farmers. I hadn't seen them since before my hospitalization. What a pathetic sight I must have been to them!

As Hank and Little John were led into their new pasture, I tried my best to smile. Even though I could only see two big, tan, fuzzy blobs, I remembered what they looked like. What a dream come true for me! My own alpacas; albeit they were the "garage sale" variety—gelded males. I wanted a bred female, but they averaged $25,000. Kim stood with her hands like a balance scale and sarcastically said, "Umm, let's see. One alpaca, or a new car. Hmmm. I wonder." Needless to say, we went with the "2 for $800" boys.

Knowing that those boys were here made my heart lighter. I was driven back down the driveway, and exhausted, put to bed for the night, even though it was only 5:30 pm.

Hank and Little John

THE MENAGERIE

Growing up in the small town of Montague, Michigan, the only animals allowed in the city limits were cats and dogs, except for my grandparent's estate. They purchased the last 80 acres in the city limits and were "grandfathered" before the law was established. They had all the cows and pigs and gardens and fields of corn that a young boy could handle—all just a short bike ride away.

After Kim and I moved back to Michigan from Yuma to teach in Lakeview, I started to want more and more animals around—beside our two boys. We moved to a great house tucked in the woods with few neighbors, some Amish and lots of state land. I put up wooden fencing in the backyard and became acquainted with the fine art of raising chickens, both meat birds and laying hens. That soon expanded to a pair of baby pygmy goats. Kim had said no to that at first, but I was smart enough to take her to the farm that was selling them. She took hold of a little baby, cradled it and said, "Ohhhhh. Get the checkbook!"

We brought home the twin girls and named them Thelma and Louise after our grandmothers and one our favorite movies. My Grandma Thelma said, "Well, I guess you named an old goat after an old goat!"

Throw in our beloved yellow lab, Joy, and several cats, I considered myself to be quite the gentleman farmer. If my Grandpa and Grandma Nelson could have only lived to see that day!

BACK IN THE DRIVER'S SEAT, WELL THE PASSENGER'S SEAT

For weeks, my time out of bed was minimal. I would be helped into a chair. I desperately wanted to read, but my vision continued to be like seeing underwater. My hearing also continued to be impaired. My voice was even affected, leaving me with a raspy, half-voice with which I could only say a couple of words with each breath.

After several weeks off work, I decided to return to teaching, much to my wife's dismay. I couldn't drive, of course, but my students were so happy to see the "rooster" return to his "chicks." My former student teacher had continued to teach marvelously and it was a seamless transition curricularly.

Every time I ran into a roadblock with teaching concepts that I used to never think about, I thought, "You can get bitter, or you can get better. Suck it up, buttercup! Now improvise!" My vision continued to be too blurry to read, so students took turns reading aloud for me. I used a digital projector with the math book to project it largely on the white board so I could see and use it. My walking remained terribly limited, so students came to my round table for assistance instead of me continuously monitoring around the room. I realized that my hearing was returning when I could hear whispering during silent reading. I thought, "Ha! I'm back in the saddle!"

When I returned to school and hobbled with my walker down the hallway or into the teacher's lounge, most of my colleagues barely said hello. I thought that was odd after all I had been through, plus, I was so excited to have returned to teaching. After my first week back, I mentioned this to my wife one evening.

"James," she began, "nobody knows what to say to you. You look and walk like a 90-year-old man. You're a shell of the person you were before your hospitalization.

You're not the person who zips up and down the hall, leaving drops of coffee as you go, talking 300 miles an hour. No one can believe that you're back at work, James, no one." Kim looked at the floor. "Hon, people don't know what to say to me either, so most of them are saying nothing at all. She looked me in the eye. "Don't be offended."

Kim's words really took me back. I thought that I looked and moved great! I was actually back to my passion: teaching and being with kids. This was where I belonged. It's all a matter of perspective.

There was a volunteer grandma, Juanita Butler, who volunteered kitty-corner from my room. She was a spry 93-year-old gal at the time who buzzed up and down the hallways, smiling all the way, and always dressed to the nines. She bounced over to my room to welcome me back and show her concern. I said, "Grandma Butler, here you are at 93 zip-dipping around the school, and here I am at 41 wobbling with a walker. What's wrong with this picture?" She giggled and waved her hand at me, "Oh, pa-shaw! You still have your sense of humor, Mr. Tanis." (Yes, she always called me Mr. Tanis, which felt weird.) She and I have laughed about that conversation many times.

FAITH STOP 5

1. What roadblocks have you encountered recently in your life? How did you manage to get through them and overcome them? What coping mechanisms did you use?

2. What are one or two of the biggest obstacles you have had to ever face in your entire life? As you look back at those stressful times, did the situations make you bitter or better in the long run?

3. Have you ever been in the situation where you didn't know what to say to someone, for example, a death? What did you do? Say something? Nothing? Please, take my advice: Even if you say something short, SAY SOMETHING! If it's uncomfortable for you, imagine the person you're considering addressing. If a face-to-face contact is too difficult, write a short note and put it in the mail. It will mean the world to that hurting and/or struggling person.

4. Read and discuss these verses together: Psalm 57:2-3, Psalm138:7-82 and Thessalonians 2:16-17.

AN EXIT BACK AND A NEW AVENUE

In April of 2008, burning nerve pain in my legs started to become unbearable again. I was prescribed Lyrica for pain and Xanax for prednisone induced anxiety. Xanax interacted with my other medication, making me terribly combative while losing control of my arms and legs. I also had slurred speech. I was like a drunken sailor! I have no memory of it, but it was pretty bad from what I hear!

After a couple of weeks on Lyrica, I started having terrible thought about myself, even entertaining suicide. This had not ever been in my line of thinking, and I had to share it with Kim. My balance also started to be really off kilter, as well as increased inflammation in my legs. We returned to the doctor and he stopped the Lyrica. This doctor suspected that I had contracted aseptic meningitis, which causes inflammation of the tissues that cover the brain and spinal cord. Other test results pointed toward various cancers, connective tissue diseases, and auto-immune diseases. He also referred me to a neurologist because of my shaky balance and abnormal gait.

An issue that also affected my job was the bathroom. When I had to go, I had to go right now. Even those muscles were greatly weakened. I did have to leave my room several times, but fortunately, the restroom was close. Although my bladder worked, my bowels did not at all. My middle stayed numb all the way through. After 17 days of nothing but a terrible gut ache, doctors wanted to perform surgery. I called Faithworks, a homeopathic center, instead. I began weekly hydrocolon therapy and massage therapy, which I continue to use to this day. The owner, Suzanne, overcame MS naturally and was "undiagnosed" after she educated herself to the natural God given medicines and homeopathic solutions. Suzanne, a strong believer, tried multiple natural therapies with me to no avail. After three years, oxygenated magnesium became available, and for the first time in a couple of years, my bowels occasionally moved on my own. I don't mean to be inappropriate, but anyone reading this who has been constipated can relate to a guy who has been chronically in this condition for years. Not a good time.

I continued to teach through different flares from August through October of 2008 and May through June of 2009. I missed virtually no work, except a few doctor appointments. My reasoning was two-fold: I wanted to honor God by being a loyal, dedicated teacher; and I loved my job and my students. The children helped distract me from the constant burning pain and numbness that continued to plague me from the waist down. I concentrated on Ephesians 2:10 which says, *"For we are God's workmanship, created in Christ Jesus to do good works, which God prepared I advance for us to do."*

In January and early February of 2010, headaches, burning and numbness in my legs and around my waist increased again. In the classroom, I would use student desks for balance. After reading a story with the students sitting around me, I stood from the chair, took one step and fell hard—right on one of my students! Fortunately, she was a tough farm girl! When asked if she was o.k., she responded, "Mr. T. it's a good thing you fell on me! I can take it! You would have crushed some of the other kids!" We all laughed it off, but I knew I was on a downward spiral.

February 11th found me back in the E. R. The doctors just shook their heads and said, "He is mystery man!" The neurologist who had seen me just laughed, shook his head and said, "I think you have a neurological disease that may be named after you!" Out of the hospital room he walked. All the doctors could say is that these flares are cyclical. No kidding. I was discharged and told to take time off work.

I was referred to Dr. Carol Beals of Beals Institute and met the woman who I call my guardian angel. Dr. Beals had a grandmotherly approach and spent five, yes, five hours with Kim and I on our initial visit. Can you imagine?

She told me that this was a partnership and she owned 51%, so I had to do what she said. She believed that I might have a neuromuscular disease that mimics MS.

From June 23 though July fourth, I experienced incredible skin sensitivity on my scalp, arms, and shoulders. It felt like a sunburn times ten. If I walked much at all, my legs began to feel like sandbags, plus those intense headaches returned. Also, my legs and arms began jerking around on their own like crazy, especially at night. This was the beginning of another month-long flare.

HOLD THE MAYO, U OF M, CAN I GET A DIAGNOSIS, PLEASE?

Sometimes when we look for answers, the best answer is that there really isn't an answer. I was given a referral to the famous Mayo Clinic, located in Rochester, Minnesota. Kim and I booked two tickets and a rental car and in August 2010, we boarded a plane to what we had hoped would be the answer. The Mayo Clinic is quite impressive looking: big beautiful buildings. I thought, "This must to be the place to get answers."

Kim and I met with a neurologist who told us that tests they would perform would be skewed because of the amount of steroids in my system. They could just make some generalized guesses. The doctor told us, "We'll do a thorough review of what's already been done." We were so disappointed that after spending thousands of dollars, no one thought to tell us that I should taper off steroids first. The only good thing that came out of it is we found a wonderful Italian restaurant, and Kim found a great merlot called J. Lohr. If you like dark reds, this is your ticket.

Next stop: University of Michigan, neurology department August 2010. I had two more hours of EMGs, where electricity was shot through my arms and legs. I was told that I should not eat sugar and I should see a headache specialist in six months or so.

Last exit: Another hospital in Grand Rapids, Michigan that has a department that specializes in neurogenic bladder and bowels. The doctor learned that we had been to Mayo and U of M and was quick to say, "Don't expect me to diagnose you."

"Doctor," I replied, "after several months, I just would like to be able to go to the bathroom on my own again." After some poking and prodding, I was told that my case was not severe enough. They worked mainly with car accident patients and things of that nature.

This challenging time brought us to our knees, asking God to help us be patient as we continued to run into costly dead ends. With time, we came to the conclusion that it was better to have no answer than for the answer to be cancer, or MS, or Parkinson's, or, or, or. We actually thanked the Lord that I did not have a diagnosis and decided to focus on pain management and quality of life.

Philippians 4:13 and 19 say, *"I can do everything through him who gives me strength." "And my God will meet all your needs according to his glorious riches in Christ Jesus."* That is Jehovah Jireh, my Provider. That is Jehovah Jireh, your Provider.

THE TERRIBLE "TILT TABLE" TEST

Dr. Beals ordered a tilt table test at yet a different hospital on August 11, 2010 to test for POTS, a rare disease where blood pools in the legs and doesn't circulate correctly. I thought, "Another day, another test." But this would be a test like none other I had to endure, one that would kill me—literally.

I arrived at the hospital and was ushered into a room with an upright table with a metal plate on which to stand. All I could think of was the old Frankenstein movies. I was asked to stand there for several minutes to see if my blood pressure would drop, which it did not. Then I was given a nitroglycerin tablet, which made me think of the Road Runner movies, and I was afraid that I was Wile E. Coyote.

It was a Friday afternoon and the doctors were bored with my lack of reaction and were off in a corner discussing their weekend plans. The nurse, however, was very professional. Suddenly I felt terribly light headed. All I said before passing out is, "Something is happening."

Something happened all right. Everything was white. I heard my name shouted over and over and it felt very chaotic. I awoke with the table tilted flat like a bed, but I couldn't move. My eyelids were cement. Eventually, I could lift them and look around. There was only a young attendant by the machine.

"Wha...what happened? I choked out, not able to control my tongue, which felt too big for my mouth.

"Dude!" the young man in the white coat excitedly exclaimed. "Your heart stopped for 14 seconds! It was so cool!"

I could hardly comprehend his words, but cool was not one I was thinking when referring to this situation. After two hours, I could finally sit up. I somehow walked unassisted slowly to the waiting room, my body feeling wooden and not my own. I wondered what I was going to say to Kim. I chose to say nothing.

"Why did that take so long?" Kim asked. "Why is your skin color greenish?"

"Oh, I just don't feel so well. I want to go home."

Ten minutes into the drive home, Kim continued to question, while my mind was mud. I finally told her that they accidentally stopped my heart. I thought she was going to drive off the road.

"What? The doctor said the test was fine and it just took a little longer!" Out came her phone and soon she was speaking with that doctor. By the time the conversation concluded, I actually felt a little sorry for that guy.

I felt absolutely awful for the next two days. I could hardly get out of bed to eat. We went to a friend's cottage on a little lake. They noticed I didn't look good and commented on it. I told them the "tilt table story," and, unbeknown to me, one of the friends was on the board of that hospital. She got on the phone too. Oh boy. The good news was that the hospital provided me with a few free sessions of acupunture, although I had to drive an hour after school to get to the hospital. However, a week later, I quickly slipped into my worst flare from which I would never recover completely.

FAITH STOP 6

1. Although James continued to battle these flares, he did not miss work until his next ER visit and doctors demanded he do so. Why didn't he call in sick? In what ways do you honor God through your work? And if you're a stay-at-home parent, you have many answers for this question, don't you?

2.   Regarding James' desire to stay in the classroom, he quoted *Ephesians 2:10, "For we are God's workmanship, created in Christ Jesus to do good works, which God prepared I advance for us to do."* How does this verse apply to you and your occupation?

3. Respond to this quote: "Sometimes when we look for answers, the best answer is that there really isn't an answer."

4. How has Jehovah Jireh been your Provider? Share specific examples.

5. Have you ever had a situation where you didn't want to completely tell your spouse/significant other everything that happened in a certain situation? (It doesn't have to be as dramatic as your heart stopping!) What was your reasoning? To protect the other person? Yourself? Is telling a half-truth telling a partial lie? Did you end up revealing everything in the end? Are you glad you did or didn't?

6. Share these verses together: Proverbs 18:9, Ephesians 4:23-24, and Isaiah 40:29.

NOT DOWN THIS ROAD AGAIN!

After my tilt table test experience, it didn't take long for my body to negatively react. On August 21, 2010, I very quickly began the onset of another flare: intense nerve pain, and that massive sunburn feeling on my back, chest, and side of arms. It was torture just to wear a light, short-sleeved shirt, and I sure didn't lean back in any chairs. The next day, my right leg was jumping and having tremors while sitting and the nerve pain was a level 9 out of 10. The following day, August 23, my right leg experienced numbness and tingling up the knee, then quickly moved to the waist, and toward chest and began to affect my breathing, while the sunburn nerve pain enveloped my entire chest and back. My gait became terribly abnormal. Kim started packing the car, and we were off to the hospital that evening.

I started a dose of solumedrol, a super steroid, and an ER doctor wanted me to consider a lumbar puncture, which I refused after previously having two, one of which leaked. I had four doctors parade in and shook their heads and walked out. The internal medicine doctor said, "This is out of my league." He reassured me the neurologist would come and see me.

I continued doses of solumedrol, and my body began to respond positively. Another internal medical doctor believed that this was an auto-immune disease that was causing the autonomic nerve dysfunction because of my response to the solumedrol. He said, "There are not tests for all auto-immune diseases, so this may be difficult to diagnose."

Before the tilt table test, I had been sent to Lansing, Michigan for two days of four hour tests called EMG (electromyogram). The purpose is to see if there were problems between the muscles and nerves. Basically, electrodes were attached to my arms and hands, and they shot electricity in higher and higher voltages. The first day was four hours on my arms, then the next day, they four hours to my legs and feet. My body was painfully jumping and twitching, and all the while I thought I was being filmed for an edition of the horror movie, *Saw*!

Now the doctors questioned the validity of the EMG that I painfully endured. I was told that EMGs are interpreted by the person administering the test, and is subjective.

I remained in the hospital for three more days and was discharged August 27th. I was discharged with the following knowledge:

1. My right side had muscular weakness and patches of numbness all the way to my knee. I could feel very little from my knee down.
2. I needed a hematologist (blood doctor).
3. My Bence-Jones protein was elevated, which pointed toward lymphomas and leukemias.
4. I probably had multiple myeloma, a cancer that starts in the bone marrow.
5. I needed to go to the Cancer Pavilion.
6. I had one of these cancers and would die in 6 months to 2 years.

This was obviously quite a blow for us. We could not get into the Cancer Pavilion for one month, so we kept this devastating news to ourselves. Can you imagine? What a burden. In these times of potential despair, I turned to the Lord and music, my first love. I played through my collection of hymnals, especially loving pieces like, "Be Still My Soul," based on the wonderful folk song, "Finlandia." I read the Word, prayed, and fasted, but music was my closest connection to God, which is true, I believe for many of us. I often sang a song to the Lord based on Psalm 61:2: *"When my heart is overwhelmed, lead me to the rock that is higher than I."* I also claimed this promise that I have posted on my bathroom mirror: *Hebrews 4:16 "Let us then approach the throne of grace with confidence, so that we may receive mercy and find grace to help us in our time of need."*

In the meantime, we worked with a wonderful neurologist who thought I should consider another lumbar puncture while I was in a flare. He consulted Dr. Beals, and they agreed that I should start immune suppressants.

Another possibility was that I had Guillain–Barré syndrome (GBS), which is an acute polyneuropathy, a disorder affecting the peripheral nervous system. Symptoms include ascending paralysis, weakness beginning in the feet and hands and migrating towards the trunk, is the most typical symptom Some subtypes cause change in sensation or pain as well as dysfuction of the autonomic nervous system. That sure sounded like me!

It wasn't until September 29th that we were seen at the Cancer Pavilion. As I held my breath seemingly forever, we were told that the Bence-Jones protein found was virtually undetectable; consequently, we should have never been told that information. We both teared up with this great news, but were angry on the drive home that we had to unnecessarily live with that awful news for a month.

I didn't have another flare until December 17th, 2010, which started with that roaming sunburn nerve pain again. Without a colonic, my bowels never worked on their own from December 31 through February 28th, if you can imagine! Terrible nerve pain ensued and numbness traveled all over my body. My neurologist ordered an MRI, which showed two lesions on my brain. To be diagnosed with MS, the magic number was now nine, plus I had fabulous reflexes, which I would not have if I had MS. Let the mystery continue.

FAITHSTOP 7

1. Think of the last time you were frustrated. What did you do to solve it? Could you do anything, or was it out of your hands?

2. As you can imagine, James and Kim were frustrated with the inability to pinpoint the cause of James' disease. Think of the word disease, which means *dis* (not at) *ease*. The body is *not at ease* when you are sick. When you are sick, do you turn to the Lord in your need? Do you just curl in a ball and ignore the world until you feel better? Discuss times in your life when you turned, or didn't, to the Lord in your time of need. What was the outcome? How would you have done things differently?

3. Discuss this verse: *"Speak to one another with psalms, hymns, an spiritual songs. Sing and make music I your heart to the Lord, always giving thanks to God the Father for everything, in the name of our Lord Jesus Christ."* *Ephesians 5:19-20* Relate this back to James' response to potential distressing news.

4. Imagine James and Kim's relief when they heard the news that cancer was not in the cards. Have you ever had a huge weight lifted off your shoulders? Did you look back at that time of trial and assess how you handled it? Did you cry out the Lord? Feel sorry for yourself? Become depressed? Consider the words of James, my favorite book: *"Blessed is the man who perseveres under trial, because when he has stood the test, he will receive the*

crown of life that God has promised to those who love him." James 1:12

5. Ponder these verses: Habakkuk 2:4, 2 Timothy 1:7, 1 Peter 5:7, and Romans 15:13.

WHAT RHYMES WITH "SCHMATERACTS?"

Kim and I, with another couple, drove to Mackinac Island to stay at the famous Grand Hotel and attend a marriage conference, which we had never done before. The conference and food were magnificent.

I was driving back home when I brushed my hand across my left eye and noticed that my vision was brownish and blurry. I thought I could see all right out of my other eye, so I didn't say anything to Kim. The blurriness continued, so I called my ophthalmologist, who knew me from my original illness when my eyesight was like looking under water. She told me to drop everything and get my yank-dank-doodle down there immediately.

I hopped in the car and she saw me quite soon. Because of my history, she was afraid of inflammation that would cause permanent damage. After her examination, she said, "Well, Mr. Tanis, there is some good news and some bad news. The good news is there is no inflammation in your eyes. The bad news is that you have a severe cataract in your right eye. You also have one in your left eye."

"How can I have cataracts? I'm too young for those!"
"Not when you have taken high doses of prednisone for as long as you have," the doctor answered,
"Ah. Another side effect of steroids of which I have not been informed."
"We will test your eyes and give you the best distance vision we can for you."

Ten years prior, I had my eyes surgically corrected with a laser. Best decision I had made in a long time. However, I was only the fourth person at this large clinic who had laser surgery and then had cataracts. There are different kinds of cataracts, I have learned. The kind that quickly developed in my eyes was the kind that turned the lenses brown. The only way to fix them was to cut them out and replace the lenses.

I went for extra special measurements and tests and finally had the right eye cataract removed. It was quick and painless. The brownness was gone, but my vision remained quite blurry. Close, but no cigar. They put the wrong lens in my eye. Does this really happen to people? Two weeks later, I had the right eye corrected again, but this time it was quite painful and blood seeped into my eye for a couple of weeks, which looked worse than it felt. A few weeks later, I had the left eye corrected.

I couldn't see to read, which included reading music, which was tricky as I was playing with my gospel band at a few churches. A couple of months had to pass to let my eyes completely heal before I could be fitted for glasses. I went from 20/20 vision to trifocals. My eyesight was one of the few things that I had left, and now that has been altered significantly, much to my disappointment. After a lot of practice, however, I almost always know which lens to look through!

LIFE IS A HIGHWAY, I WANNA RIDE IT ALL NIGHT LONG

Kim and I had to wrap our heads around the fact that I very well would not come to a diagnosis. Kim is a "solver" and a "fixer", so this was difficult for her to accept. My goal became clear: what can I do to improve my quality of life. I am in my early 40s and cannot imagine living like this for another 40 years.

After talking with my auto-immune specialist, Dr. Beals, about my desire to improve my quality of life, I was prescribed a huge regimen of pharmaceuticals, such as neurtonin and amitriptyline for nerve pain, a medicine used for Parkinson's that stopped the leg tremors, azathioprine, an immune-suppressing drug often used for cancer, which would hopefully stop my body from attacking itself, plus a plethora of others, which I collectively call, "My second breakfast."

My quality of life did improve, with some "tweaking" of medicine levels, and implementing homeopathic remedies as well as weekly hydrocolon therapy. Praise the Lord, my life remained relatively normal, albeit with a new, much lower baseline, for nearly two years.

I asked the school board for a medical leave of absence for a year, which they granted. After one year, I knew I could not stand for more than ten or fifteen minutes. Sitting is not one of the things an elementary teacher does often! I asked the school board for a second year medical leave, which they graciously granted.

I had to adjust to my new role as a stay at home dad, but I was sending everyone to school and staying home alone. It was a terribly difficult adjustment for me. I was "the breadwinner," after all. O.K., Kim and I made the exact same amount, but as a male, I felt this inherent need to provide for my family.

I had to learn to provide in a completely different way: pack lunches, do dishes, make dinner, do laundry, go shopping, and clean house. Wow! Talk about a paradigm shift! I eventually learned to enjoy my new role and thank the Lord that I was still able to serve and honor Him and my family in a different capacity.

SEIZURE TIME, BREAK IT DOWN

Brrrrr. I had been cold for almost two days. It was the end of January 2013, so that normally would not be unusual, but I just could not get warm. I went to bed with my nose as cold as my dog's and I even put the covers over my head.

After a restless night, I decided to get up and take a bath at 4:45 am. I started the bath, stood up, and thought, "Gosh, I'm light headed. Wow, I'm so nauseated." And that's the last I remember. Too bad Kim can't say the same.

Kim heard a terrible crash and came running to the bathroom. I was lying on the floor, shaking from my bloody head to toe, not really breathing. Time stood still. Should she start CPR? Call 911? After a few frantic minutes to find her phone and four attempts to call 911, she was speaking with an emergency responder.

Living in the sticks has its advantages, but this is a disadvantage: needing an ambulance in a hurry. I sort of "came to" during the 25-minute wait, and cried about how much my head hurt. Later we surmised that I hit it on the corner of a cabinet, the vent handle, the tub, and the tile floor. I always say, "Go big or go home!" I lost control of my bladder and was still plagued with head to toe shaking.

The ambulance arrived and I was slipping in and out of consciousness. I recognized one of the EMTs because she used to be a paraprofessional at my school. We did not see eye-to-eye on, well, just about everything. As they sat me up on the toilet seat, I remember thinking, "I hope she doesn't give me a "swirly!"

Although they were virtually whispering, everyone's voices seemed so loud as I continued to fight to stay conscious. Apparently, I told them I did not need their help to the ambulance. They put a hard plastic "turtle shell" around me in case of spinal injury and carried my sorry self to the ambulance. I don't remember the ride, and did not start to stay cognizant until I had been admitted to the hospital.

As it turns out, I had pneumonia, and I did not know it. That, coupled with two medicines for steroid-induced hypertension, caused an abnormal drop in my blood pressure. I ended up staying two days in the hospital, which is a record short time for me.

I had not been hospitalized for two years, and thought that now I was free and clear for at least another two. Although I felt much better, I still did not feel quite "back to baseline." As usual, I ignored it and tried to live life. I had been designing two rather large stained glass windows for our church that were to be dedicated to a few saints that had "been promoted to Glory." I focused my attention on these windows and finished them in only 35 hours. There was a nice dedication made during church, with many of the family members in attendance. My youngest son, Jacob, helped me install them that week above the original wooden doors of the 125-year-old "Little House on the Prairie-type" church in the country.

In the middle of March, I even was able to paint my bathroom from the dreaded sage to a warm milk chocolate and sand down the vanities in two bathrooms and stain them black.

Cross Window

Dove Window

PARKING THE CAR, HANDING IN THE KEYS

The time has come, the Walrus said, To talk of many things:
Of shoes and ships and sealing-wax, Of cabbages and kings.
And why the sea is boiling hot, And whether pigs have wings.
–Lewis Carroll

Two years of a medical leave came and went, and I knew in my heart of hearts that it was time for me to give up the ghost. I had such a passion for teaching and my students consistently did well on local and state assessments. I just couldn't believe that all of my experience working in the classroom, 15 years participating on Michigan State Department of Education committees developing state assessments, the professional development that I taught, and all the stuff! Tubs and tubs of units and pattern blocks and book sets and art supplies—one half of our pole barn was dedicated to my teaching supplies!

I have had to go through a mourning process regarding my career and all that I had accomplished. "The time has come, the Walrus said, to talk of many things…" I now had to talk about a letter of resignation. With many tears, and mainly Kim's help, this is the letter that was crafted and submitted to the Superintendent and the school board:

Tuesday, February 19, 2013

Dear (Principal), (Superintendent), and Board of Education,

It has been a great pleasure that I have been employed as a teacher with the our school since August of 1996, and I have been honored to serve students, parents, and community members alike. Many students have touched my life and blessed me with their smiles, stories, and kindness. Some of the most compassionate and exemplary staff members are employed in this district, and I have enjoyed having the opportunity to work with them. Indeed teaching is a great profession, and I have found it to be most rewarding. I feel privileged to have been called to the profession of education as both my parents and wife have been.

Unfortunately my health will not allow me to serve any longer in the classroom again. Although teaching has been my great passion, I will now use my gifts and talents in other capacities. I wish to thank all of you publicly for the opportunity to teach for this fine school district. A special thank you to those who have supported me over the years and have somehow touched my life in a positive manner.

Please, respectfully accept my official resignation.

Sincerely,

James A. Tanis

I officially closed the door on that chapter of my life. I never thought that would happen at age 45. I know that when God closes a door, He opens a window; I just hope the devil didn't caulk it shut.

THERE'S NO PLACE LIKE THE HOSPITAL FOR THE HOLIDAYS
March 17th 2013 (St. Patrick's Day) through March 31st (Easter)

I was leaving an icy driveway of a friend with some guys in late March of 2013. One friend, standing next to me asked if he should help me to my car. I waved him off, "I'm fine," then did the splits and hit the ground. It didn't hurt, and we laughed as he insisted on getting me situated in my car. My shoulder hurt a bit the next day, but I was otherwise fine.

On March 15, I woke up and could not feel or move my left leg, which was my "good" one. It wasn't tingly or anything, just a dense numbness to my hip. I was sure I had pinched a nerve from that fall because I have some warning when I have a flare and there is always a more gradual rise of numbness with pain and tingling.

I went to the chiropractor and had an adjustment, and the next day the numbness moved up to my waist. March 17th was a big day in our family. I would be five years to the day that I was first taken to the hospital. Even though we are not Irish, we make a big corned beef dinner and buy cheesy sparkly green necklaces to celebrate my triumph over death. I also needed to play for church and directed the choir that morning, which Kim let me do.

After our nice dinner, Kim convinced me to have an MRI of my lower back to look for a pinched nerve. I begrudgingly agreed and tried to ignore the luggage she was putting in the car. That afternoon ER visit resulted in a typical midnight hour MRI that showed no pinched nerve and I was admitted, regardless of all my sputtering and muttering.

I was moved to the Neuroscience floor, which also has folks with dementia and other mental problems, so there were some weird incidences after the sun went down! I could not get out of bed without a lot of assistance, and I could not sleep between the high amounts of steroids and the all night checking on me and prodding and poking. I slept three hours in 48 hours and thought I was losing my mind.

An IV of solumedrol, a super steroid, was begun, and I was given a gram a day for five days, which is a huge amount. In the past, my body had responded to solumedrol. This time would not be the case. After three days with zero response, my wife and I asked the neurologists about the treatment called plasma exchange. We had researched it previously, and had been interested in it, but it was terribly expensive. After five days of solumedrol and no results, the neurologists agreed to this treatment, and I smiled for the first time since being there.

To have plasma exchange, I first had to have a short surgery to place a double port in my jugular. The doctor said. "You will feel pressure three times," and was he right: push! Push! PUSH! The eight-inch tube went directly to my heart. It didn't hurt so much, but felt uncomfortable. That night, however, I had an awful, deep ache that medicine didn't touch. I stayed up literally the whole night.

A nurse came in the next morning at 8:30 am with the plasma pheresis (exchange) machine. Her name was Mary, and she was very kind and explained the procedure to Kim and me. While I turned my head to the left, she cleaned the two ports and connected two tubes to the machine. When it began, it sounded like an Amish sewing machine, then it got somewhat louder.

My blood was going out one port, being spun in a centrifuge, and the lighter weighted yellow plasma with the bad antibodies was going into a bag. Simultaneously, my red blood was being warmed up and circulated back into my body with a human derivative of plasma pharmaceutically mixed with saline called albumin. It didn't hurt at all, and the whole process took about one and a half hours.

The objective was to remove my plasma that carried the antibodies in my blood that were attacking my own system. The process consists of five treatments, with a day of rest in between treatments. I figured that the way the schedule fell, I would not finish treatments until after Easter!

I had agreed to direct a choir at another church in town to get them through Easter and no one else could even play the music! What was I to do?

I had my oldest son, Zechariah, bring in his keyboard and computer and all the music. Even though I had one finger attached to a machine measuring my oxygen level, he digitally recorded all the music for me and even altered my mistakes when my taped up finger sometimes slipped off a key. He then emailed the files to the pastor, who had the choir practice the Wednesday before Easter. Problem solved, right? Wrong. The practice was a disaster, and the choir just didn't want to perform the songs without me there. I felt terribly guilty, of course, but I was stuck in the muck. The pastor came to visit me to reassure me that they just picked out some great Easter hymns and practiced them instead. He smiled and said, "If we can do all your songs by Pentecost, it would be great."

After he left, I was distraught over this situation, but tried to look at the bigger picture. I prayed that God would let me at least have two treatments two days in a row without a day of rest. Then I would finish my last treatment on Easter day, and potentially go home. I continued to pray in earnest toward this end, even though the neurologist said it would not happen.

That evening, a nurse came in with a puzzled look on his face. For reasons unexplained, there was a change in the schedule and I was to receive my second plasma exchange tomorrow without a day in between. I was grinning and I told him that I knew why.

The next day, a nurse named Emily came in and introduced herself. I said, "I knew I would see you today! I prayed this would happen!" She smiled and said, "Wow. Now there's some faith." That opened the door for me to witness to Emily, who believed in God. We had a great conversation about his faithfulness, and she said that she would be back on Easter for my last treatment.

"Well, you know we're going to have us some church, Kim, you, and me."

"I can't wait," Emily responded. "Because it's your last treatment, I will do yours first We can try to schedule the removal of your port and see if we can get you home for Easter."

Easter morning arrived, and Emily, true to her word, showed up at 8:30 am.

"Ready for your last treatment?"

"Ready for some church?"

Emily laughed and brought in the plasma pheresis machine. After I was attached and running, I read the crucifixion and resurrection stories from Matthew, Mark, and Luke. We listened to some great videos on YouTube, like "I Know My Redeemer Lives," by Nichole C. Mullen. Then we had some marvelous prayer time together. We parted friends with eternal connections. What a glorious Easter service the three of us had!

The plasma exchange ended at 10:00 am, and I was scheduled to have the port removed at 11:00 am—talk about divine timing! As I was being wheeled away to a different floor, I hollered to Kim, "I'm off to be 'deported'!" The transport folks had never heard that one and repeated it to everyone they could. The port removal procedure was explained to me by a nurse, who would be the one actually removing the port.

"Let's practice our breathing, on my instructions," the nurse began. "Big breath in, breathe out. Breathe in, breathe out. Big breath in-and he pulled that eight-inch tube out!

"Don't breath yet." He propped up the head of my bed. "Now breathe out," he said, and he put painful pressure for ten minutes on the hole. It felt like having a ginormous sliver being pulled out of my chest. Amazingly, after ten minutes, the bleeding had virtually stopped. While he was applying the pressure, I told him that I wanted to see the port, which he showed me after he taped up the hole. I looked at amazement at this long plastic tube that was in my jugular just minutes before.

"I've been deported!" I cried and back to my room I was wheeled to a nervous Kim.

"Everything went smooth as silk," I reassured Kim. After a few hours to make sure that the hole in my neck would not bleed anymore, the doctor began discharge papers. Before it was all said and done, Kim and I were driving home before dark on Easter Sunday. Yet another prayer had been answered.

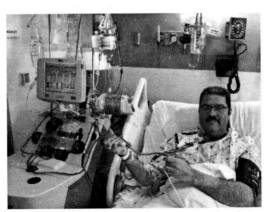

"Bye-bye yellow plasma and antibodies,
Hello albumin and my blood!"

TWO HOLY SPIRIT INTERCESSIONS

I must testify to the very tangible work of the Holy Spirit two times during the first five days of this hospitalization. The first was on the third night. As usual, I wasn't sleeping, even though it was around 2:00 am. I was lying on my back, twiddling my thumbs, all hopped up on steroids.

I started to smell this nice, sweet aroma. It wasn't sugary, but more flowery. I had no flowers in my room. My sense of smell became more acute as this beautiful aroma filled my room. I knew without knowing why, deep in my spirit, that it was the Holy Spirit comforting me. I just smiled, breathed deeply, and let the Comforter bless me. My body relaxed more and I enjoyed His ministering for approximately 30 minutes. I eventually fell into a deep sleep, my first since being hospitalized.

The fifth night, I had another, very real encounter with the Holy Spirit. I was lying on my back, as usual, and it was the middle of the night and I was wide awake, again. I felt a hand on my back, then several hands, all over my back.

"How can this be?" I whispered. "I'm lying on my back, how can I feel hands on my back?" It was not scary; it was comforting. I continued to feel these hands moving all over my back for 20 minutes. The hands were distinct and were of different sizes. The hands were gently applying pressure, just as someone would who was laying hands on you would do.

I just whispered, "Thank you, Jesus," and remained still and let the Holy Spirit minister to my body again. I could feel my body relaxing as hands joined in and other hands moved. Could it be angels ministering to me? I'm sure it could have been. I just accepted the aid that I needed during those times.

Romans 8:26-27 says, *"In the same way, the Spirit helps us in our weakness. We do not know what we ought to pray for, but the Spirit himself intercedes for us with groans that words cannot express. And he who searches our hearts knows the mind of the Spirit, because the Spirit intercedes for the saints in accordance with God's will."* All I know is that both of these Heavenly encounters happened when I was wide awake. I have never before had this happen, and I know that I must testify to the goodness of the Lord's help and mercy in my time of need.

FAITHSTOP 8

1.　After the seizure and subsequent hospitalization, James tried to begin regular activities as soon as he could, even if he did not feel too well. Why did he do this? Was this a wise thing to do? What should he have done instead?

2.　James really thought that his numbness was just a pinched nerve. Have you ever had something that you thought was a smaller problem that turned out to be much larger instead?

3.　James became quite distraught when he knew he could not fulfill his obligations for Easter. Although he tried to fix it the best he could, the "best laid plans of mice and men" just didn't pan out. Have you ever tried to fix a situation and been frustrated by not receiving the outcome you expected? What did you do?

4.　Have you ever focused on a small problem without seeing the bigger picture, like James did with the Easter music? Did someone or God have to tap you on the shoulder to get you to see that you needed to let it go?

5.　What do you think of the Tanis' 2013 Easter? How does one's outlook make a situation better or worse?

6.　What is a situation where you had to look at the glass half full or half empty? Which did you choose? How did it affect your attitude and possibly the outcome?

7.　Ponder this verse: *"In the same way, the Spirit helps us in our weakness. We do not know what we ought to pray for, but the Spirit himself intercedes for us with groans that words cannot express. And he who searches our hearts knows the mind of the Spirit, because the Spirit intercedes for the saints in accordance with God's will."* **Romans 8:26-27** What are your thoughts regarding James' two encounters with the Holy Spirit? Is he crazy? Dreaming? Can these accounts be true? If so, what can that mean for you and your spiritual journey?

8. Look up these verses and discuss: Exodus 23:25, Psalm 147:3, Isaiah 58:8, Jeremiah 30:17, James 5:14-15, and 1 Peter 2:24.

THE TRAVELS CONTINUE

Kim and I continue this new adventure back to health. Since that Easter Sunday, the road to recovery took time. I was discharged with a cool blue "tricked out" walker that included a seat, which I used for a month before graduating to a cane. Each week I was regaining about 10% feeling in various patches on my left leg, which means the plasma exchange was working. With this returning feeling came severe burning nerve pain. By noon most days, it was all I could do to distract myself from the constant pain, which I did with prayer and reading of the Word and other Christian resources. My toes still remain numb, except for my big toe, which is a blessing since I need that toe the most for balance.

I also developed strange blister-like sores on my scalp and face for about a month. I remember thinking, "This is very Job-ish." My guess was that it was just more inflammation presenting itself and leaving my body. Through prayer and supplication Kim and I continue to ask the Lord for the strength to live in the victorious life that is promised to all believers.

"Jesus bore our sickness on the cross, by whose stripes we were healed." 1 Peter 2:24

I believe this verse is for our physical sickness and our spiritual sickness. This means that we need to let the past go. We are no longer bound to that guilt; it was nailed to the cross. You have been justified. Justified means it is just as if you haven't sinned! As far as the East is from the West--Let it go!

I began a blog that shares this story, but also is connecting people from all over who are plagued with undiagnosed auto-immune diseases. There are also pages of natural remedies and homeopathic solutions that have blessed me, and I hope will also bless others who may not be familiar with them. The blog continues to expand with stained glass pictures and fun DIY (Do It Yourself) ideas.

Please visit my blog, share on your Facebook page, and e-mail. Encourage others to share this blog so that more people with auto-immune diseases can come together in a common community.

Visit: msdisease.weebly.com**
as well as
Facebook/james.tanis.94
and
<u>jamestanis@live.com</u>

I would enjoy hearing from you! ☺

**On December 23, 2013, James <u>was finally diagnosed with MS</u>. Of course, he doesn't have any of the "normal indicators," which made his case so difficult to pin down. MS is an auto-immune disease with varying degrees of symptoms. Please share this book and website information with any folks you know who have MS also.